It has been a joy throughout m[...]
ladies I look up [...]
My Mom, Grandmas, [...]
Recipes have been tasted, loved, and shared through many generations and
there is no end to the art, joy, and love of cooking!
I hope you enjoy this collection of recipes as well as my Mic-Tips throughout
the book!
Whether you are preparing Brunch, Lunch, Dinner, or
Dessert there is something special in here for you, your family, and friends!

Love,
Michaela
Brown

Contents

Brunch   4

Lunch   14

www.StageToTheStove.com

Contents

MICHAELA BROWN

116 Central Ave NE
Le Mars, IA 51031

Designed
Photographed
Written
by Michaela Brown

BRUNCH

Lemon Poppy Seed Loaf

1 box lemon cake mix
1 pk. lemon instant pudding
4 eggs
½ c. vegetable oil
1 c. water
3 Tbl. poppy seed
Mix together cake and pudding. Add eggs, water and oil. Beat 4 minutes.
Stir in poppy seeds. Pour into greased pan, 2 loves or 1 Bundt pan.
Bake 45 minutes at 350°.

Breakfast Pizza

Spread 2 tubes of crescent rolls on a 12' pizza pan. Forming a thin layer and thick crust around the edge. Bake at 350° for 15 minutes or until golden brown.

Filing:

8 eggs

½ c. milk

1 c. shredded cheese

1 lb. sausage, cooked

Whip together eggs and milk. Add cheese and sausage. Pour into crust and bake at 350° for 20 minutes or until thoroughly cooked. Serve hot.

Michaela Brown

Apple Snow Balls

4 baking apples (Macintosh)
1 Pkg. instant maple & brown sugar oatmeal
8 tsp. water
1 – 6oz cup vanilla yogurt

Wash apples and remove the top of the core and all of the
seeds to make a small hole in the middle of the apple. Cut a
line around the middle of each apple, just piercing the skin.
Place in a baking dish and fill each apple with 2 tsp. of
maple & brown sugar oatmeal and slowly pour 2 tsp. of
water over oatmeal. Bake at 350° for 20 minutes. Remove
from oven and place a spoonful or two over the top of
apples. Add a cranberry or serve it plain. Serve hot.

Spiced Fruit Salad

15 oz. can sugar free peach halves
15 oz. can sugar free pear halves
10 oz. can maraschino cherries
2 Tbl. Lemon juice
15 cloves
2 sticks cinnamon (broke in half)

Drain juice from fruit into a saucepan. Add lemon juice., cloves and cinnamon sticks. Simmer for 20 minutes. Meanwhile arrange drained fruits in a bowl or individual serving cups. Pour hot syrup over fruit, Top with cinnamon sticks. Cool, then chill overnight in the refrigerator.

Keep yokes centered in the eggs by stirring the water while cooking hard-boiled eggs. Especially good for deviled eggs.

Michaela Brown

Sausage Quiche

1 (9 inch) pie shell
1 pound sausage
4 eggs
2/3 c. milk
¼ tsp. salt
dash of cayenne pepper
1 ½ c. sharp cheddar cheese, grated
¼ c. red peppers, diced
¼ c. green peppers, diced

Partially bake pie shell at 400° for 10 minutes. In a large skillet, cook sausage and crumble; drain well. In a medium mixing bowl, combine eggs, milk and seasonings; beat together. Sprinkle half of the cheese over the baked pie crust and top with sausage. Slowly pour egg mixture over sausage. Sprinkle other half of cheese over the sausage and spread the peppers over the top. Bake at 350° for about 35 minutes or until eggs are set.

Candied Bacon

1 lb. thick cut bacon
½ c. brown sugar
2 Tbl. yellow mustard

Slowly cook bacon and drain fat. Mix sugar and mustard. Drizzle over the bacon. Remove from pan and place on serving platter.

Almond Rhubarb Coffee Cake

1 ½ c. brown sugar, packed
2/3 c. corn oil
1 egg
1 tsp. vanilla
2 ½ c. all-purpose flour
1 tsp. baking soda
1 tsp. salt
1 c. milk
1 ½ c. rhubarb, chopped
½ c. almonds, sliced
½ c. powdered sugar
1 Tbl. butter, melted
¼ almonds, sliced

Preheat oven to 350°. Grease two 9-inch round cake pans. In a large bowl, beat brown sugar, corn oil, egg and vanilla until smooth. In another bowl, mix flour, baking soda and salt. Add to first mixture alternately with milk. Beat until smooth. Stir in rhubarb and almonds by hand. Pour batter into prepared pans. Mix powdered sugar, melted butter and almonds in a bowl. Sprinkle over batter. Bake 30-35 minutes or until a pick inserted comes out clean. Cool.

Michaela Brown

Purple Ribbon Shortbread

1/2 cup butter, room temperature
1/3 cup powdered sugar (unsifted)
1/4 teaspoon vanilla
1 cup flour (unsifted)

Cream the butter in an electric mixer or with a wooden spoon until it is light. Cream in the powered sugar and vanilla. Slowly work in the flour. Mix dough until combined and mixture is nice and smooth. Spray the shortbread pan very lightly with a non-stick cooking spray. Put the ball of dough in the middle of the pan, and working from the center, firmly press the dough into the pan. Prick the entire surface with a fork. Bake at 325° for 30-35 minutes, or until it is lightly browned.

This shortbread recipe won a purple ribbon in the Round Barn when I was quite young, and then years later in 4-H, won another purple ribbon and a trip to the Iowa State Fair!

Fruit Pizza

Crust: 1 c. Sugar
2 ½ c. flour
1/4 tsp. salt
1 c. butter, softened
1 egg
1 tsp. vanilla
1 tsp. baking powder
Mix together and pat onto a large pizza pan. Bake at 350° until golden brown.
Filling: 1 (8oz) pkg. cream cheese, softened
1 c. Cool Whip
½ c. powdered sugar
Mix well and spread on cool crust. Top with fresh fruit of your choice. Alternating colors for prettiest look.
Strawberries - Blackberries - Blueberries - Kiwi- Raspberries

For a low calorie alternative, use lite cream cheese and substitute yogurt instead of Cool Whip.

Mic-Tip

Michaela Brown

Scalloped Pineapple

1 c. (1 lb. 4 oz) pineapple
½ c. butter
1 c. sugar
5 slices bread, cubed
4 eggs
Melt butter, add eggs, sugar, cubed bread and pineapple. Bake in a 9x9 inch pan for 1 hour at 350°

For quick and perfectly sliced strawberries, cut off the stem and slice in an egg slicer. Great for a quick ice cream, shortcake, yogurt or angel food cake topper!

LUNCH

Caesar Salad with Pasta

1 head green leaf lettuce
½ cup caesar salad dressing
Shredded mozzarella cheese
Croutons
1 c. cooked pasta (fancy noodles)

Bring 4 cups of water to a boil and cook past till tender, about 7 minutes. Drain and let cool. Cut head of lettuce into bite size pieces and place in a medium bowl, add in dressing , cheese, pasta and toss till lettuce is covered. Add croutons to top and serve.

The easiest and best way to flavor your pasta is while it is cooking. Add a teaspoon of salt to your boiling water before adding the pasta.

Nacho Cheese Soup

2 lbs. hamburger
1/3 block of Velveeta cheese
2 cans minestrone soup
I can chili beans
1 can Rotel tomatoes (original or mild)
1 can chicken broth

Brown the hamburger. Then add the Velveeta cheese and stir until melted. Add remaining ingredients. Serve hot.

Garlic Flat Bread

Brush both side of the flat bread with olive oil and sprinkle with garlic salt. Place in a preheated broiler for about 30 seconds on each side. They brown fast and burn quick, so keep a close eye on them!! Cut into pizza shaped slices and serve warm.

Michaela Brown

Black Bean, Corn and Tomato Salad

1 - 29 oz. can black beans
4 plum tomatoes, quartered
salt to taste
1 – 29oz. can corn kernels
½ c. green onion
½ bunch cilantro, chopped
juice of 1 lime
¼ c. olive oil
black pepper to taste
cayenne pepper to taste

Drain black beans and corn. Quarter tomatoes and salt to taste. In a bowl mix black beans, corn, and onion and mix well. Add the cilantro, lime juice and olive oil and stir to coat. Season with salt, black pepper and cayenne pepper. Pour into serving dish, add tomatoes around the edge. Serve immediately or let stand for 30 minutes to blend the flavors.

Lunch

6 Layer Salad

Dressing:
1 c. Miracle Whip
1 Tbs. apple cider vinegar
5 Tbs. half and half
3 Tbs. sugar
Whip together all ingredients till smooth. Set aside.
Salad:
1 head of lettuce
1 c. peas, frozen
½ c. green onion, finely chopped
½ c. bacon, cooked and finely chopped
1 c. shredded cheddar cheese
Remove core from lettuce head and cut up lettuce and place the bottom of a 9x13in pan. Spread dressing evenly over the lettuce. Spread remaining ingredients in layers, peas, green onion, bacon and cheese over the lettuce and dressing. Chill until served.

Michaela Brown

Oriental Coleslaw

1 (3 oz.) package oriental ramen noodles
½ cup olive oil
3 tablespoons sugar substitute
1 tsp. pepper
¼ apple cider vinegar
½ head cabbage, chopped
1 c. silvered almonds
2 Tbls. sunflower seeds
2 green onions, chopped

Combine the seasoning packet from the ramen noodles, oil, sugar, pepper and vinegar in a bowl and whisk till well mixed. Mix the cabbage, almonds, sesame seeds and green onions in a bowl. Add the ramen noodles, reserving a few for garnish, if desired. Add the dressing to salad. Toss to mix and top with the remaining noodles.

Mic-Tip

To keep your salad fresh on the serving table, try this....
After washing the salad, place a saucer upside-down in the bottom of the bowl. The excess water drains off under the saucer and keeps your salad fresh and crisp!

From The Stage To The Stove

Veggie Pizza

Spread 1 tube of crescent roll dough out on a 12' pizza pan and bake at 350° for 10 minutes until golden brown. Cool.

Filling:
1 (8oz) pkg. cream cheese, softened
1 c. Miracle Whip
1 pkg. Lipton dry vegetable soup mix
Mix and spread thickly on crust.

Top Layer:
Use whatever combination you like!
Carrots - Celery - Cauliflower - Radishes - Onion - Green Pepper
Broccoli - Ripe Olives - Mushrooms

Top with shredded cheese for a different twist and added flavor!

Michaela Brown

Strawberry Spinach Salad and Homemade Dressing

1 Tbl. olive oil
2 tsp. vinegar
½ tsp. cinnamon
1 tsp. lemon juice, fresh squeezed
1 Tbl. honey
1 bunch spinach
¼ c. green onion, sliced
1 pint strawberries, sliced

Wash and cut off the spinach leaves. Toss in onion and strawberries.
Mix remaining ingredients together and pour over the spinach leaves.
Serve right away.

DINNER

Poppyseed Chicken

2 lbs. chicken
8 oz. sour cream
1 can cream of mushroom soup
3 Tbl. poppy seeds
1 sleeve Ritz crackers
1 stick butter, melted

Cut chicken into bite size pieces and brown in frying pan. In a bowl, mix together sour cream, cream of mushroom soup and 2 Tbl. poppy seeds. Add chicken to soup mixture and pour into a 9x9 baking dish. Crush Ritz crackers and add melted butter. Pour over chicken and sprinkle with remaining poppy seeds. Bake at 350° for 30 minutes.

Dinner

Mic-Tip

When preparing a casserole, make an additional batch to freeze. Just remove from the freezer and bake in the oven. You never know when you will need an emergency meal if an unexpected guest arrives!

Lasagna

2 lb. ground beef	¼ c. grated Parmesan cheese
1 onion (chopped)	2 eggs
1 Pkg. Lasagna noodles	2 c. mozzarella cheese
1 24 oz. jar pasta sauce	2 tsp. dried parsley
26 oz. cottage cheese	

In a large skillet over medium heat sauté the onion in 1 Tbl. butter add the ground beef and brown. Drain the grease. Add pasta sauce and simmer for 5 minutes. Meanwhile in a large pan bring 4 quarts of water to a boil. Add pasta and cook for 12 -15 minutes. Drain water from noodles. In a large bowl, mix together the cottage cheese, 1 1/2 cups of the mozzarella cheese, eggs, grated Parmesan cheese, dried parsley, salt and ground black pepper. To assemble, in the bottom of a 9x13 inch baking dish evenly spread 3/4 cup of the sauce mixture. Cover with 4 lasagna noodles, 1/3 of the cheese mixture, and 1 cup sauce. Repeat layers twice. Top with noodles, remaining sauce, remaining mozzarella. Bake in a preheated 350° oven for 45 minutes. Uncover and bake an additional 10 minutes. Let stand 10 minutes before serving.

Dinner

Make each slice of your lasagna look beautiful when served! Cut a tomato into thin slices and add to the top of the

Mic-Tip

Michaela Brown

Parmesan Pull-A-Parts

3 Tbs. butter
1 Tbl. minced onion
1 tsp, garlic powder
1 tsp. poppy seed
¼ tsp. celery seed
1 can biscuits
¼ c. grated parmesan cheese

Melt butter and add garlic powder, onion, poppy seed and celery seed. Separate biscuits and cut into fourths. Roll biscuits in butter mixture then roll in Parmesan cheese. Place biscuits in a pan starting in the middle and working outward. Bake at 400° for 15 – 18 minutes.

Blueberry Party Salad

1st Layer: 1 pkg. raspberry jello   2 cup hot water   ¼ tsp. blueberry flavor
Add raspberry jello to hot water and stir till dissolved.
Pour into a 9x13 in. pan and chill till firm.

2nd Layer: 1 envelope plain gelatin   1 cup sugar   ½ cup cold water
1 tsp. vanilla   1 cup half and half   1 8 oz. pkg. cream cheese – soft
½ cup chopped nuts

In a medium bowl, soften the gelatin in the cold water. In a pan heat the half and half and sugar until hot but not boiling. Place all ingredients in a bowl, expect the nuts, and blend until smooth. Stir in nuts. Cool. Pour over the first layer and chill until firm.

3rd Layer: 1 pkg. raspberry Jello   1 -15 oz. can blueberries
1 cup hot water   ¼ tsp. blueberry flavor

Dissolve the gelatin in the hot water. Pour in the entire can of blueberries, including the juice, and flavoring. Cool. Pour over the 2nd layer and chill. Cut into squares and serve.

Chicken/Asparagus Roll-Ups

4 chicken breasts, split, skinned, boned and pounded thin
Salt and pepper to taste
1 lb. fresh asparagus
2 Tbl. all-purpose flour
1 clove garlic, minced
1 tsp. salt
½ tsp. thyme
¼ tsp paprika
2 c. sliced white onions (cut ¼ inch thick)
3 large tomatoes, sliced ½ inch thick
½ c. chicken broth

Season chicken breasts lightly with salt and pepper. Place 2-3 asparagus on each chicken breast half. Roll up tightly; secure with toothpicks, if necessary. Set aside. Combine flour, garlic, ½ tsp salt, ¼ tsp thyme and paprika. Roll chicken in this mixture. Place half of onions and tomatoes in bottom of 9 x 13 inch pan. Place chicken breasts over vegetables; top with remaining onion and tomato slices. Combine broth with remaining salt and thyme; pour around chicken. Cover pan loosely with foil. Bake at 350° for 30 minutes, basting every 10 minutes. Uncover and bake until tender, about 10-15 minutes.

Dinner

Michaela Brown

Lobster Newburg

6 baked puff pastry shells
Newburg Sauce
2 cups diced cooked lobster

Preheat oven to 350°. Make Newburg Sauce. Stir in the lobster and cook over simmering water until the lobster is heated through. Spoon the mixture into the baked pastry shells, replace tops and bake at 350° for 15 minutes.

Newburg Sauce

3 Tbl. butter
½ tsp. salt
3 Tbl. flour
1/8 tsp. pepper
1 c. hot milk
½ tsp. paprika
dash of cayenne
2 egg yolks, lightly beaten
¼ c. cream

In the top of a double boiler melt the butter over low heat. Remove from heat and stir in the flour, salt and pepper. Add the hot milk, return to the heat and cook, stirring, until the sauce is thick. Stir in the paprika, cayenne. Beat the egg yolks and cream together lightly and mix into sauce.

Juicy Lucy Burgers

2 lbs. hamburger
6 slices of cheese
salt and pepper to taste
6 hamburger buns

Take a small amount of hamburger and make it into a thin patty. Take a slice of cheese and tear it into quarters and arrange in the center of the hamburger patty, leaving room around the edge. Make another thin patty and place on top of the half with the cheese. Pinch the edges together and then round it into a nice hamburger shape. Salt and pepper to taste. Place on the grill and cook for approx. 6 minutes on each side. Times may vary with each grill.

Try adding more to your Juicy Lucy than just cheese!
- Sautéed onions
- Cooked bacon bits
- Blue Cheese, Swiss Cheese, Pepper Jack

Michaela Brown

Cheese Texas Potatoes

1   2lb. package frozen hash brown potatoes
½ c. chopped green onions
¼ tsp. pepper
1 tsp. salt
16 oz. sour cream
1 can cream of chicken soup
10 oz. shredded cheddar cheese
bacon bits (optional)
1/4 c. melted butter

Combine first 7 ingredients in a 9x13 inch pan. Sprinkle with bacon bits and additional cheese if desired. Drizzle with butter. Bake at 350° for 1 hour.

Mic-Tip

Marinating is easy if you use a plastic bag. The meat stays in the marinade and it's easy to turn, rearrange. For clean up, just toss the bag!

Rhubarb Slush Punch

6 c. chopped fresh or frozen rhubarb, thawed
7 c. water
1 ½ c. sugar
¾ c. thawed orange juice concentrate
¾ c. thawed lemonade concentrate
10 cups 7-up

In a large saucepan, bring rhubarb and 4 cups water to a boil.
Reduce heat and simmer, uncovered, for 5-8 min. or until rhubarb
is tender. Mash rhubarb, strain. Reserve juice and discard pulp.
Add sugar, concentrates and remaining water to rhubarb juice.
Transfer to a freezer container and freeze. Remove from freezer
30-45 min. before serving, scraping the surface as it thaws. Place
equal amounts of slush mixture and 7-up in each serving glass.
Serve immediately

Always chill juices or
sodas before adding to
beverage recipes.

Mic-Tip

Michaela Brown

Orange Glazed Cornish Hens

3 Rock Cornish Hens
2 Tbl. butter, melted
½ c. orange juice
1 Tbl. honey
½ tsp. salt
¼ tsp. dry mustard
1/8 tsp. paprika

Place hens, breast side up, on a rack in shallow roasting pan. Brush with melted butter. Roast uncovered at 350° for 30 minutes.

Prepare glazed oranges. Mix together remaining ingredients. Brush half of the orange juice mixture over the hens. Roast uncovered, brushing with remaining orange juice mixture, until hens are done, about 45 minutes longer. Cut each hen along the backbone from tail to neck into halves with kitchen scissors. Serve with glazed oranges.

Glazed Oranges

3 oranges
2 Tbl. butter
¼ c. light corn syrup
1 Tbl. honey

Cut off ends of oranges. Cut each orange into 1/8 inch slices. Heat butter in a 12oz. skillet over medium heat until melted. Stir in corn syrup and honey. Heat to boiling. Add oranges and reduce heat. Simmer uncovered, spooning sauce frequently over oranges, until oranges are tender and glazed, about 25 minutes.

Country Fried Steak Meal

4 cubed steaks
2 c. flour
Salt
Pepper
5 large potatoes
1 bag of carrots
1 pkg. Lipton's dry onion soup mix
1 c. water

Pour flour into a Ziploc bag. Salt and pepper cubed steak. Put steak inside bag with flour and turn upside down until steak is completely covered with flour. Place meat into a large skillet with grease and lightly brown on each side. (discard remaining flour.) Peel potatoes and carrots. Cut into small chunks and place in a casserole dish. Lightly salt and pepper. Place lightly browned cubed steak over the top of potatoes and carrots. Sprinkle dry onion soup mix over the meat, potatoes and carrots. Pour in water. Cover with tin foil and bake at 400° for 1 hour or until potatoes and carrots are tender.

Dinner

Michaela Brown

Cream Cheese Corn

1 8oz. package of cream cheese
½ stick, butter
32oz. bag, frozen corn
salt & pepper to taste

In a large pan on medium heat, melt butter and soften cream cheese.
Add the bag of frozen corn and cook for 10-15 min, or until hot.
Stirring occasionally. Add salt and pepper to taste before serving.

Crock Pot Corn
- Place all ingredients
in a crock pot on
low-med heat out of
the way! Try
doubling the recipe
for large parties!

Stuffed Pork Tenderloin

1 pork tenderloin (6-8 servings)
1 6oz. box Stove Top Stuffing Mix
1 ½ c. water
¼ c. vegetable oil
1/2 c. flour
1 tsp. salt
1 tsp. pepper
1 tsp. oregano

Mix together Stove Top mix, oil and water in a medium size bowl and microwave on high for 5 minutes. Fluff with a fork and set aside. With a sharp knife, filet the pork tenderloin till "flat". Spread stuffing mix over the tenderloin, roll up and tie with string to hold secure. Mix together flour, salt, pepper and oregano in a shallow dish and roll the tenderloin, covering completely. Sear each side on med-high heat in a large skillet. Pace in pan and cover. Cook for 1 hour at 350°. Remove from oven and let stand for 20 minutes. Slice into serving size pieces and cover with cream sauce. Serve right away.

Cream Sauce

1 can Cream of Mushroom Soup
½ c. heavy whipping cream or half and half

Place can of soup in a blender and blend till smooth. Place in a med size pan on low/med heat. Add cream and cook until bubbly. Stirring frequently.

Michaela Brown

Carrots Supreme

1 onion, sliced
2 Tbl. butter
2 chicken bouillon cubes
1 lb. carrots
1/8 tsp. salt
2 Tbl. sugar

Brown onions in butter. Dissolve bouillon cubes in 3/4 cup hot water. Add carrots and bouillon to onions. Sprinkle with salt and sugar. Simmer, covered, until carrots are nearly tender (approx. 40 min.). Uncover and simmer allowing excess liquid to evaporate (approx. 10 min.).

Sausage & Apples

2 Tbl. butter
1 large onion
1/2 c. apple jelly
1/2 c. firmly packed brown sugar
2 lbs. little smokie sausages
3 apples, peeled, cored and sliced
1 Tbl. cornstarch
2 Tbl. warm water

In a large skillet, melt the butter and add the onion. Saute on medium heat until onions are golden.
Stir in apple jelly and brown sugar. Add sausages and reduce heat to medium low. Cook, stirring occasionally for 20 minutes.
Add apples, partially cover pan and cook for 10 min. or until apples are tender. Combine cornstarch and water, stir into pan. Cook 2 to 3 minutes or until mixture thickens. Serve warm.

Dinner

36   *Michaela Brown*

- Crush crackers in plastic bag and add melted butter right to the bag for quick and easy preparation and cleanup!

- Thaw all meats in the refrigerator for maximum safety.

- To prevent cheese from sticking to a grater, spray the grater with cooking spray before beginning.

- When serving bread or rolls, place aluminum foil under the napkin in your basket and the rolls will stay hot longer.

- Shredded carrots – If your shredding carrots for a dish, why not shred extra and place in a small container with a wet paper towel over top to hold in moisture. Use for salads or garnishes.

- To keep hot fat from splattering, sprinkle a little salt or flour in the pan before frying.

- Remember to remove the tops of carrots before storing. Tops drain the carrots of moisture, making them limp and dry.

- Keep adding leftover veggies (corn, peas, green beans, etc.) from meals, to a medium size container in your freezer. When the container is full add the veggies to you broth for a quick vegetable soup. You can also add chunks of chicken or beef to make it a chicken/beef & vegetable soup!

DESSERTS

Cream of Coconut Cake

1 white cake (white cake mix)
1 15 oz. can cream of coconut
1 tub cool whip
1 1/2 c. coconut, toasted

Prepare white cake mix according to the instructions on box. Cool.
Take a knife and cut holes all over the cake. Pour cream of coconut
slowly over cake so it soaks into the holes. Top cake with cool whip
and toasted coconut. Chill until served.

Strawberry Rhubarb Pie

2 cups sliced rhubarb
2 cups halved strawberries
1-1/4 cups sugar
1/4 cup MINUTE Tapioca
1/4 tsp. vanilla
1/4 tsp. almond flavoring
1 Tbl. butter
2 pie crusts

Preheat oven to 425°F. Mix rhubarb, strawberries, sugar, tapioca, vanilla and almond flavoring in large bowl. Let stand 15 minutes. Place 1 of the pie crusts in 9-inch pie plate. Fill with fruit mixture; dot with butter. Cut second pie crust into 6 (1-1/2 inch-wide) strips with pastry wheel or knife. Place 3 of the strips over filling. Weave lattice crust with remaining strips by folding back alternate strips as each cross-strip is added. Fold trimmed edge of lower crust over ends of strips. Seal and flute the edge by crimping around the crust with your fingertip and knuckle. Bake 45 minutes or until juices form bubbles that burst slowly. Cool.

Desserts

Michaela Brown

Pie Crust

2 1/2 cups all-purpose flour
1 tsp. salt
1 tsp. sugar
1 cup unsalted butter, cut into pieces
4-6 Tbl. ice cold water

Mix the dry ingredients together in a medium-size bowl. With a fork or pastry blender cut in the pieces of butter until the mixture resembles coarse meal. Add 4 tablespoons cold water, work with your hands until dough comes together. If the dough is still crumbly add more water one tablespoon at a time. Do not overwork the dough! Divide the dough in half and form into disks and wrap separately in plastic wrap. Refrigerate for 1 hour. To form the pie shell, roll out the dough into a 14 inch circle on a lightly floured surface. Gently place the circle into a 9 inch pie plate and trim a 1 inch overhang.

Desserts

For flakier pie crusts, add 1 teaspoon of vinegar to the cold water in preparing your pie dough.

Mic-Tip

- Make the dough the day before and let it rest for 1 hour refrigerated after rolling and shaping to prevent distortion and for the best shape.

- Does your cherry pie always soak through the bottom crust and make it soggy? Place a baking sheet in the preheated oven for 15 min at 400 degrees. Then bake you pie on the baking sheet. The heated baking sheet will heat the bottom crust faster so it is baked and flaky coming out of the oven!

- For the best baking results, use a glass or dull-metal pie pan. Avoid shiny metal or disposable aluminum pans, which reflect heat and prevent crusts from browning. Dark pans may cause crusts to brown too much.

- To keep baked edges from getting too brown, cover the edges with foil after the first 15 minutes of baking.

Michaela Brown

Old-Fashioned Butterscotch Pie with Meringue

2 Tbl. butter
¾ c. brown sugar, firmly packed
1 ¾ c. hot milk
¼ c. cold milk

¼ c. cornstarch
pinch of salt
2 egg yolks
1 tsp. vanilla
1 baked 9 inch pie crust

Meringue:

4 egg whites
½ tsp. cream of tarter
pinch of salt

¼ c. sugar
2 Tbl. cold water
½ tsp vanilla

In the top of a double boiler, melt butter; blend in brown sugar. Cook directly over medium heat, stirring, until mixture is bubbly; watch carefully that it doesn't burn. Slowly stir in hot milk and place over double boiler again. Cook, stirring, until blended. In a small bowl, blend together cold mild, cornstarch and salt. Stir into hot mild mixture and cook, stirring for 1 to 2 minutes or until thick and smooth. Cover and cook for 10 minutes, stirring occasionally. Beat yolks lightly and stir in some of the hot mixture. Blend thoroughly and stir back into top of double boiler. Cook, stirring, for 3 minutes. Remove from heat. Stir in vanilla and beat until smooth. Let cool to room temperature, stirring occasionally, then pour into pie shell and spread evenly.

Meringue:

In mixer, beat together egg whites, cream of tarter and salt until moist peaks form. Very gradually beat in sugar, then water and vanilla, beating until mixture is shiny and stiff. Spread evenly over filling, making sure meringue touches pastry all around edges. Swirl top of meringue decoratively. Bake at 375° for about 12 minutes or until meringue is brown.

Desserts

From The Stage To The Stove

Kuchen Dough

1 cups milk
1 cup water
1 pkg. yeast
½ cup sugar
½ cup shortening (lard)
5 cups flour
2 tsp. salt

Dissolve package of yeast in warm water and milk. Add sugar, shortening, salt and flour to make soft dough. Knead. Divide dough into four 6-7oz. balls.

Dough can be used for caramel rolls too! Makes two 9x13 in pans.

Michaela Brown

Kuchen Filling

1 cup milk, half & half or sweet cream
½ cup sugar
1 heaping Tbl. flour
1 egg, beaten
1 tsp. vanilla

Blend sugar, flour and egg together and add milk. Cook in a saucepan on medium low heat until thick like custard. Stirring occasionally. When thick, remove from heat; add vanilla and blend. Roll out one ball of Kuchen dough and form in a 8-inch pie plate. Pour filling into crust. Bake on bottom rack of oven at 325° for 20 to 25 min. or until golden brown. Cool and serve.

Mic-Tip

Variations for toppings include placing peach slices over the top with a sprinkle of cinnamon or nutmeg. Cherry pie filling spread across crust and dotted on filling. Blending ¼ cup ground poppy seed with the filling. Canned, dried or fresh apricots, peaches or prunes.

Poppy Seed Rolls

Filling:

3 cups ground poppy seeds

3 cups sugar

½ tsp. salt

2 heaping Tbl. flour

2 eggs, beaten

2 ½ cups half and half

2 tsp vanilla

Grind the seed and pack into the cup. Place all the ingredients except the vanilla in a saucepan and cook on medium high heat until it is bubbly, stirring constantly. Remove from heat. Add the vanilla. Roll out 1 ball of Kuchen (page 44) dough into a 12 x 15 x ¼ in rectangle. Spread with 1 cup filling and roll up like a jelly roll. Seal the ends and edges carefully so filling won't leak out. Put in greased pans and let rise for 30 min. Bake at 350° for 20 min. our until top is light brown. Filling makes enough for 4 poppy seed rolls.

Bulk poppy seed is sometimes hard to find. So you can use two 12.5 cans Solo Poppy Seed filling. Eliminate the sugar and salt from the mixture since it is already added to the can.

Michaela Brown

Carrot Cake

2 c. self-rising flour
2 c. sugar
4 eggs
1 c. oil
2 c. grated carrots
1 tsp. vanilla
2 tsp. cinnamon

Mix all ingredients together. Grease and flour two 8-in or 9-in round layer pans. Divide batter into the two floured pans and bake at 350° for 20-30 minutes or until golden brown.

Icing:

½ stick margarine
2 c. confectioners sugar
8 oz. pkg. cream cheese
2 tsp. vanilla

Mix until smooth with no bumps. Layer the cooled cakes with a small amount of icing between layers. Frost the outside. Add crushed pecans to the top and sides as desired.

Caramel Apple Pizza

2 medium apples, thinly sliced
1 Tbl. lemon juice
1/2 cup sugar
2 tsp. cinnamon
1 tsp. nutmeg
1 package (3 oz.) cream cheese
1 large egg
1 package (17 1/4 oz.) frozen puff pastry
1 c. chopped nuts
Caramel Syrup (page 49)

Heat oven to 400°. Line 2 cookie sheets with aluminum foil. Prepare caramel syrup. Toss apples and lemon juice in a medium bowl, stir in the sugar, cinnamon and nutmeg.

Beat cream cheese with an electric mixer on medium speed until fluffy, add egg and vanilla and beat until blended.

Roll each sheet of pastry into a 10 inch square onto the baking sheets. Spread half of cream cheese mixture over each pastry. Arrange apple slices onto the squares, sprinkle with nuts. Drizzle about 1/4 cup syrup over over each square. Bake 25 to 30 minutes or until puffy and golden brown. Pour remaining syrup over pizzas. Serve hot.

Michaela Brown

Caramel Syrup

1/2 c. plus 2 Tbl. packed brown sugar
1/3 c. corn syrup
2 Tbl. butter
1/3 c. whipping cream
1 tsp. vanilla extract

Heat brown sugar, corn syrup and butter in 1 quart size saucepan over medium heat until boiling, stirring constantly until thick. Remove from heat. Cool slightly, stir in whipping cream and vanilla extract.

Mic-Tip

Ripen peaches, pears, and tomatoes quickly by placing them in a brown paper bag with a ripe apple. Set in a cool, shady spot and make sure there are a few holes in the bag. The ripe apple gives off a gas, ethylene, which stimulates the other fruit to ripen.

Glazed Pineapple on the Grill

1 pineapple
3 Tbl. brown sugar
3 Tbl. honey
½ tsp. cinnamon

Slice pineapple in ½ inch slices. Mix together brown sugar,
honey and cinnamon. Place pineapple slices on the grill and
spread a small amount of honey mixture on the pineapple. Grill
for 2-3 minutes. Turn pineapple and repeat on the other side.
(Pineapple may be peeled before grilling if preferred)

Michaela Brown

Chocolate Soufflé

2 squares unsweetened chocolate
3 Tbl. butter
2 Tbl. flour
¼ tsp salt
1 c. milk
½ c. sugar
1 tsp. vanilla
4 egg yolks
4 egg whites, stiffly beaten
½ c. heavy cream, whipped stiff

Preheat oven to 350°. Butter a 2-quart soufflé dish and sprinkle the bottom and sides with granulated sugar. Mix together the chocolate and butter. Blend in the flour and salt to make a smooth paste. Gradually add the mild, sugar and vanilla, and cook, stirring constantly, until thick and smooth. Remove from heat and cool slightly.

Add the egg yolks and beat well. Fold in the beaten egg whites and pour into the soufflé dish. Set in a pan of hot water and bake at 350° for about 45 minutes. Serve warm, with the whipped cream served separately.

Strawberry Patisserie

1 pkg. puff pastry sheets
1 egg (for wash)
1 pkg. white chocolate instant pudding
1 c. milk
1 c. heavy whipping cream
1 lb. fresh strawberries, sliced
2 Tbl. apricot preserves
2 Tbl. water

Heat milk, cream and white chocolate pudding in a small saucepan over medium heat. Remove, and chill until cooled and set. Cut puff pastry sheets along folded lines and lay out 4 sections. Cut ¼ inch strips out of the last two sections. Place two small strips on the edges of the larger sections to form a boarder. Brush with egg wash. Bake at 350° for 25-30 min. or until golden brown. Remove, using a spoon, press down the middle of each section, leaving a boarder on the edges. Let cool. Using a piping bag or spoon, fill the pastry shells with white chocolate mixture. Top generously with sliced strawberries. Cut each section in half and serve.

Michaela Brown

- Want to know how to get and easy, beautiful glaze like you see on a French Patisserie?
Place 2 Tbl. apricot preserves, 2 Tbl. water in a small saucepan and cook until it is in liquid form. Brush over top the pastries. Chill until glaze is set.

- Only grease bottom of pan... you couldn't climb up a greasy pole could you?!!

- If the top of your cake is browning too quickly, place a pan of warm water on the rack above the cake while it is baking in the oven.

- Brown sugar will not harden if stored in the freezer.

PARIS

Paris was my DREAM and Music is my PASSION!
"From the Stage to the Stove" pretty much sums up
what I love to do!
Years ago my dream of going to Paris, France to cooking
school at the Le Cordon Bleu Culinary Institute came true.
My trip and culinary training was an experience I will never
forget, and I'm excited to share it with you!

THANK YOU!

TO MY FAMILY FOR BEING SUCH A HUGE HELP,
INSPIRATION AND FOR ALL YOUR GREAT IDEAS!
TO ALL MY FAVORITE COOKS -
MOM
GRANDMA HAAR
GRANDMA BROWN
GRANNY
GRANDMA PITTENGER
GRANDMA GINNY

Proverbs 31:15

She rises also while it is still night,
And gives food to her household.....